Original title:
A Dance with the Squid

Copyright © 2025 Creative Arts Management OÜ
All rights reserved.

Author: Simon Fairchild
ISBN HARDBACK: 978-1-80587-304-4
ISBN PAPERBACK: 978-1-80587-774-5

In the Ink's Embrace

In waters deep, where currents play,
A creature glides, in a strange ballet.
With flailing arms, it twirls around,
Dancing clumsy, yet joyfully profound.

Its ink flows out, a swirling plume,
Creating patterns that light the gloom.
With every twist, and every spin,
It trips on its limbs, wears a goofy grin.

Tentacle Tango

Tentacles twirl, no rhythm found,
A slippery dance on the ocean's ground.
With wobbly steps and splashes loud,
It invites the fish, a quirky crowd.

They spin in circles, a fishy career,
As bubbles burst and laughter's near.
With a twist and a turn, they jive away,
In the watery hall, they frolic and sway.

Whispers of the Deep Sea

In the dark below, giggles abound,
As creatures gather from all around.
A shimmery flash, a secret shared,
Of charming moves, they've all prepared.

With silly faces and playful pouts,
They sway and sway, amidst watery shouts.
The waves join in, a playful cheer,
As every flipper brings forth a jeer.

Choreography of Chitin

Under sea foam, crabs take the stage,
With dances wild, they earn their wage.
A shuffle here, a scuttle there,
Each one competing for the fish's stare.

Their shells clink loud in a rhythmic beat,
As barnacles clap with tiny feet.
In a quirky show, they strut with flair,
While octopuses giggle, swinging in midair.

Beyond Waves: Entwined Hearts

In the brine where laughter swirls,
Tentacles twist and giggles twirl,
A splash of joy and ink so bright,
What a sight, oh what a sight!

Bubbles rise with silly tales,
As jellies dance and seaweed sails,
With every flip, we're all aglow,
In this wacky ocean show!

Rubber ducks join in the fun,
Splashing round, oh what a run!
Kraken winks with cheeky grace,
In this underwater race!

So grab your fins and dive right in,
Let the ocean games begin!
With foamy waves and silly cheer,
We'll dance beneath, no hint of fear!

Tranquil Meets in Mystic Waters

In the calm of seafoam green,
A dancing fish, a sight unseen,
With every flip and gleeful spin,
The ocean grins, let the fun begin!

Squid and turtles twirl around,
Creating waves, a laughter sound,
They bump and glide, wave after wave,
In the playful depths, so brave!

What a sight, the sea's parade,
In colorful hues, their jokes are played,
With each new flicker, a new surprise,
Beneath the blue, oh how time flies!

So gather round, young and old,
For tales of waters brave and bold,
With every ripple, joy is found,
In this dance of laughs, we are unbound!

Undercurrents and Euphoria

In the ocean's fun swirl, they twirl so bright,
Their tentacles waving, a comical sight.
Clad in colors that shimmer, they giggle in glee,
While dodging a crab who's just lost his key.

With a splash and a plop, they leap and they dive,
These goofballs of water, so happy, alive.
They wear hats of seaweed, no style's too absurd,
In the currents they frolic, like no other herd.

Movements in the Mariana

In a trench deep and dark, where no sun has shone,
They dance 'round a rock, feeling right at home.
With awkward pirouettes and a jiggle or two,
They sing underwater, a cephalopod crew.

A bubble of laughter rises up to the light,
As they twirl with the sand, what a glorious sight!
The fish give them side-eyes, but they don't really care,
For the deep sea is theirs, and they're quite the fair.

Rhythm of the Abyss

With a flap and a flop, they groove to the sound,
In the darkest of depths, where weirdness is found.
They whirl through the algae, a hilarious mess,
Each snap of a tentacle, causing distress.

Clapping their suckers to a jellyfish tune,
Creating bright ripples under the moon.
They invite all the crabs to a jubilant fest,
Where the rhythm of laughter is truly the best.

Cephalopod Serenade

In a kelp forest glade, they sway like a breeze,
With their quirky expressions, they aim to please.
Their colors keep changing, like moods on parade,
Making fish giggle, all scales half displayed.

With a wink of an eye and a flip of a fin,
They embark on adventures, where laughs never thin.
From the shallowest shoals to the deep dazzling blue,
These jolly creatures dance, like they always do.

Sinfonia of the Sea

In the briny depths they sway so free,
A jiggly symphony for you and me.
With wiggly limbs that tickle and tease,
They spin and twirl, as if to please.

Bubbles rise like notes in the air,
A giggly chorus beyond compare.
Their ink squirt parts the water's sheen,
Creating laughs in this underwater scene.

Fluidic Fantasia

In currents swift, they glide and slide,
These charming creatures, what a wild ride!
With suction cups that pull you near,
They spin you 'round, you'll squeal with cheer.

A wobbly jig, a silly ballet,
Tentacles twirl in a playful display.
With a splash and a twirl, they steal the show,
Who knew the sea could be such a pro?

Tentacles in Harmony

Eight arms a-waving, oh what a sight,
A wild frolic, day turns to night.
With twists and turns, a giddy spree,
In rhythm with waves, oh joyous glee!

A whirl and a giggle, they prance about,
Tickling fish with a friendly shout.
Their joyful jig makes the sea grass sway,
Together they laugh, in their own silly way.

The Ocean's Enchanted Minuet

In silken tides, they frolic and glide,
A merry jig that won't be denied.
With each little flop, there's laughter galore,
In this watery waltz, who could ask for more?

Glistening like jewels, they dance on the reef,
Their silly moves bring giggles and grief.
As seaweed sways to their playful tune,
The ocean erupts in a chuckling swoon.

Echoing Elegy of the Deep

In depths where shadows play,
A wiggly snack sways,
With eight flailing arms,
It dances all day.

Bubbles rise, laughter bursts,
Tentacles flail in thirst,
Fish peek through a window,
This party's well-rehearsed.

An octopus in disguise,
Waves and giggles arise,
Doing the wobbly twist,
Oh, what a surprise.

Bright colors swirling round,
In this watery ground,
They shimmy through seaweed,
A spectacle is found.

Undulating Tales of the Tide

Giggling crustaceans join,
As the squid strikes a pose,
With a wriggle and a whirl,
Oh, how the fun flows.

Jellyfish play the drums,
While the shrimp tap their feet,
Stars above just twinkle,
To this quirky beat.

A splash here, a dash there,
Underwater ballet,
The squid shakes its arms,
Like it's having a day.

They twirl in the brine,
Creating chaos in glee,
Kelp sways to the rhythm,
In this bouncy sea.

Vivid Tidescape

A canvas made of blue,
With laughter splashed around,
A squid brings the jazz hands,
As silliness is found.

Cuttlefish join right in,
In a whirl of bright hues,
Dancing past the coral,
While the starfish snooze.

With giggles that echo,
Through bubbles and tides,
The swirling sea monsters,
Have nothing to hide.

They caper and giggle,
In a comical spree,
Creating a ruckus,
Beneath the wild sea.

Celestial Sea Cha-Cha

A shimmy and a shake,
Among the neon glow,
The squid leads the charge,
In a gleeful show.

Turtles clap their flippers,
As the bass drums resound,
Whales are crooning loudly,
In this underwater ground.

Gusts of laughter bubble,
Through the salty mist,
A ballet of the tides,
That can't be dismissed.

With glimmers and giggles,
In a joyous ballet,
The sea creatures whirl,
In their playful display.

Fluid Elegance

Tentacles twist in wild delight,
With a wiggly spin, they take flight.
Each graceful move, a silly sight,
As fish watch on with pure delight.

Suction cups clinging, they glide around,
In a watery ball, without a sound.
They pirouette and tumble bound,
Creating chaos where fun is found.

The Twilight Waltz

Beneath the waves where shadows creep,
A creature stirs from restful sleep.
With floppy feet and jumps so steep,
It rocks the boat, no time for sheep!

Glowing limbs in colors bold,
Twirling tales that never get old.
A jolly jig of stories told,
In currents calm, this dance unfolds.

Pulses of the Ocean Floor

With every pulse, the ground shakes free,
A cephalopod joins in with glee.
It dances low, then high like a spree,
Playing hide and seek, oh who could it be?

In waving kelp, it spins and swirls,
A friendly wave to all the pearls.
The rhythm speeds, round and round it whirls,
Inviting laughter from fishy girls.

Luminous Lullaby

In the moonlit depths, a glimmering friend,
Bounces and giggles 'til the very end.
With each squishy move, expectations bend,
A light-hearted jig, no need to pretend.

It sways like a jelly with jelly-filled dreams,
Floating grace amidst bubble beams.
In this funny world, nothing's as it seems,
A serenade of laughter that bubbles and streams.

Shadows Twisting in the Abyss

In the depths where shadows play,
Tentacles twist in a silly ballet.
With a wobbly glide and a splashy spin,
They laugh as they tease the small fish within.

Underwater giggles bubble and burst,
As each little critter gets caught in the thirst.
With glimmers of laughter where seaweed sways,
The cephalopods dance in whimsical ways.

Scripting the Sea's Movements

Bubbles rise with a cartoonish flair,
As squids write scripts in the salty air.
With ink as their pen, they scribble and swirl,
Crafting comedies in a watery whirl.

The audience of fish is so easily wowed,
At the squids' antics, they cheer and they crowd.
With a squirt and a wink, they leave them in awe,
As they dance 'neath the waves, without any flaw.

Dancers in the Coral Kingdom

In the realm where colors burst bright,
Squids tango with corals, a comical sight.
With a shimmy and shake, they twirl round and round,
In a lively parade of mischief profound.

Anemones chuckle, waving their fronds,
As squids show their moves, with rhythm and bonds.
A burlesque of bubbles, a frolicsome glow,
Turning the ocean into a lively show.

Mysterious Turns Beneath

Beneath the ripples, the secrets spin,
As squids play hide and seek with their kin.
With twists and with turns, they flash here and there,
Creating giggles that dance through the air.

In the depths lie the jokes only they can see,
With a squirt of ink, they burst like confetti.
Mysteries of laughter spread far and wide,
As they whirl in the waters, their glee can't be denied.

Embracing the Tentacled Whisper

In aqua blue, they twist and sway,
Flicking limbs in a silly display.
A wobbly jig in the salty air,
With suction cups everywhere!

They tickle toes with a playful tease,
Silly antics bring giggles with ease.
Round and round, they whirl and spin,
What a show this ocean has been!

The Lurid Lull of the Sea

Bubbles pop with a splashing sound,
As creatures dance all around.
A giddy glide through the briny mist,
With wriggly friends, none can resist!

Octopi spin, and fish take a dive,
Making mischief, they're so alive!
With every ripple, a laugh they share,
In this watery world, no room for despair!

Dwelling in the Currents

In currents swift, they weave and laugh,
Taking turns in a gleeful path.
Clumsy flips and whimsical bows,
With every somersault, laughter grows!

Galumping around in a jiggy swirl,
Wobbly tails like a spinning pearl.
The sea's a stage for a zany show,
Where waving tentacles steal the show!

Paths of the Sea Spirits

With shimmering fins and glittering scales,
They shuffle about with magnificent tales.
A comical crew in the ocean's embrace,
These tiny dancers bring smiles to the place!

From quiet depths to bubbly shores,
Their frolicking joy simply soars.
Playing hide and seek in the coral maze,
In humorous splendor, they amaze!

Synchronized Swirls

In ocean's depths, where silliness thrives,
Creatures twirl in mismatched jives.
Tentacles twist like playful flags,
As underwater chums wear silly rags.

Bubbles burst, creating a show,
With every swirl, they steal the flow.
A clownfish giggles at the sight,
While seahorses join the zany flight.

Tangled limbs and jovial grins,
Who knew that sea life could be such wins?
With every twist, they share a laugh,
In this watery world, fun is their craft.

So dive on in, let laughter spread,
Join the antics where humor's bred.
A splash of joy in waves so grand,
In the depths where silliness stands.

Seagrass Soirée

Under the waves, what a sight to behold,
Seagrass sways, inviting the bold.
Crabs in bowties, clams wearing hats,
Celebrating life with squeaks and spats.

The starfish tap dance, oh what a treat,
While jellyfish glide on their squishy feet.
A conch shell sings out a tune so spry,
While the mermaids giggle and wave goodbye.

Dolphins are dancing, leaping with glee,
The quirky sea turtles join in the spree.
With bubbles and laughter rising like foam,
In this garden of sea, they feel right at home.

So raise a fin, let the laughter resound,
In this soirée where fun's always found.
Beneath the waves, what joy to see,
The underwater party of pure jubilee!

Vortex of Vibrant Motion

Swirling colors in the ocean bright,
Creatures spinning in pure delight.
Twirling and whirling like a funfair ride,
In this lively whirlpool, there's nowhere to hide.

Octopuses giggle, arms all a-twist,
Trying to tango, but they just can't resist.
With a blink and a swirl, they tumble and fall,
Creating a splash that attracts them all.

Fish follow suit, darting in glee,
Joining the chaos beneath the sea.
As they spin and dip, no room for despair,
In this vortex of fun, all swims with flair.

So come take a dip in this vibrant maze,
Where laughter and joy always amaze.
In the riptide of fun, we'll dance and glide,
In this oceanic swirl, come join the tide!

Abyssal Ballet

In the depths where shadows play,
Creatures gather for a grand display.
Waltzing with currents, they twist and twine,
In their whimsical world, everything's fine.

With a wink and a flick, an eel takes the lead,
As a pufferfish pouts in its spiky bead.
The flatfish slides in a graceful sweep,
Creating a rhythm, they dive and leap.

With a swirl of tentacles and a flip of a fin,
They twirl and twiddle, letting the fun begin.
In the abyssal glow, they glide with grace,
A spectacular show in this magical place.

So join the ballet of the sea's silly crew,
Where laughter and whimsy are all we pursue.
In the depths of the ocean, where we are free,
Let's take part in this dance, just you and me!

Choreography of the Darkened Waters

In shadows deep, they twist and twirl,
Eight legs in sync, a wiggly whirl.
Tentacles waving, what a sight!
A slippery ballet in the moonlight.

With a splash and a giggle, they glide,
Inks of color, a slippery ride.
They trip on rocks and bump a fin,
Laughter bubbles as they spin.

Each twist, each turn, a comical show,
Muddled steps steal the spotlight's glow.
A fish joins in, just for the fun,
As bright as the sun, till the dance is done.

When the curtain falls on deep-sea glee,
They bow together, all fancy-free.
The ocean chuckles, waves in delight,
In darkened waters, their humor's bright.

In the Company of Ink

Inksplash parties on coral floors,
Squid and friends knock on seaweed doors.
They play hide-and-seek in sea foam wigs,
Who knew the ocean had such funny gigs?

With silly hats of old clamshells,
They crack jokes that give fishy spells.
A wink, a squirt, laughter unbound,
In the company of ink, joy is found.

Slimy routines that make them topple,
Each one flops like a gooey bobble.
Ink blots dance in a vibrant spree,
What frolicsome shapes, oh, come and see!

In swirling currents, they leap and dive,
A portrait of joy, so alive.
With ink as their muse, they skip and prance,
In the sea's great hall, they twirl and dance.

The Aquatic Masquerade

Underwater masks, tucked snug and tight,
Creatures prance about, what a whimsical sight.
Winking eyes peer from every nook,
As seaweed skirts sway like a storybook.

Clams in tuxedos, crabs wearing crowns,
Each one dancing through seabed towns.
Fish giggle loud, bubbles rise high,
While electric eels light up the sky.

The orchestra plays with a clunky beat,
Clattering shells and vibrations sweet.
A barnacle plays the maracas right,
As everyone twirls till the morning light.

As twilight fades, the masquerade ends,
With hearty laughs and squishy friends.
Under sea stars, in shimmering shades,
They carry home dreams from this grand parade.

Serenade of the Silken Clutch

Beneath the waves, a serenade flows,
Squid in sequins, striking a pose.
They croon soft tunes with a squelchy flair,
As shimmering bubbles drift through the air.

Pulling off tricks with a comedic grace,
Twisting around in an inky chase.
One floats too high, then lands with a thump,
The audience roars, as the sea creatures jump.

With harmonies tugged from the deep's heart,
They laugh and twirl, each playing their part.
In waves of giggles, they shake and shudder,
An underwater concert, full of splutter.

At curtain call, with a splash and a cheer,
They gather close, their joy sincere.
With fins and flashes, they exit the stage,
Leaving behind tales of their inky rage.

Embrace of the Ocean Shadows

In the depths, something wiggles,
A creature with eight floppy giggles.
It ties my legs in a silly knot,
As I splash and flounder, laughing a lot.

With ink clouds swirling all around,
I dodge the bubbles like a clown.
Oh what a sight, this cephalo parade,
A wobbly jig, an aquatic charade.

Tentacles tickle, oh what a game,
Each twist and turn, never the same.
I try to swim, but I slip and slide,
In this underwater joyride.

With friendly waves and laughter loud,
We make a motley, dancing crowd.
In shadows deep, we twirl and spin,
Who knew the ocean could be such a win?

Pulse of the Deep Gelatin

In the chilly blue, a jello surprise,
A wiggly thing with big, glimmering eyes.
It wobbles and bounces with comical flair,
I can't help but giggle as it floats through the air.

Tentacles waving like silly balloons,
Moving in rhythm with whimsical tunes.
It wraps around me, a playful embrace,
We're both just two goofballs in this fun space.

Bubbles erupt, it's a slippery mess,
Every splash brings me joyous distress.
Gliding and sliding, oh what a ride,
As this jiggly partner becomes my guide.

From polka-dots to stripes in bright hues,
We craft our own dance, with every move.
In gelatin dreams, we bounce like a frog,
Two oddball friends in a fantastical fog.

Dance of Bioluminescence

Beneath the waves, it starts to glow,
A bright little flash, like a friendly show.
With sparks and twirls, it lights up the night,
Promising giggles in the shimmering light.

With every zap, it pulls me near,
This glowing buddy brings festive cheer.
We bounce and we twist in the ocean's dome,
Creating a party beneath our foam.

Like fireworks firing in blues and greens,
Our underwater shenanigans burst at the seams.
Each flicker a laugh, each shimmer a grin,
How could such fun come from under my fin?

With every swirl, we dance and play,
Lighting up the sea in a magical way.
Together we giggle, our joy set free,
In this grand underwater jubilee!

Embrace of the Cephalopod

Down in the briny, a rascal appears,
With eight squiggly arms and plenty of cheers.
It pulls at my toes with ticklish delight,
As we whirl and twirl in the dim ocean light.

Each grip is a giggle, each tug a surprise,
Bright colors swirling like wild fireflies.
We twist like spaghetti, all tangled and lost,
In this quirky embrace, we never count cost.

Doing the cha-cha with a wink and a jig,
This lovable mischief, oh, I can't help but dig.
With each little nudge and enthusiastic spin,
We craft silly stories with laughter within.

As bubbles rise up, we kick and we sway,
In the embrace of this friend, I'll always stay.
Together we jest, in this watery world,
Two playful souls, like flags, unfurled.

Spinning Tales of Tentacles

In the ocean's wide embrace,
Eight arms wriggle and race,
With each twist, a jellyfish giggles,
As the octopus juggles in little wiggles.

A crab joins in for a snappy beat,
While fish laugh and wiggle their feet,
They spin tales of pranks, oh what a sight,
As bubbles pop in the warm moonlight.

A cottage of shells becomes their stage,
As they frolic and wriggle, free from cage,
The sea anemones sway to delight,
While seahorses dance, oh what a night!

With laughs echoing far and wide,
In their wacky world where secrets hide,
These ocean friends, quirky and bright,
Spin tales of joy, a true fishy fright!

The Dance of the Abyss

In the depths where shadows play,
Creatures frolic, night and day,
A turtle teaches moves so slow,
While an eel gives a zippy show.

Grumpy fish try not to frown,
As a sea star twirls, a little clown,
The squid takes charge, with style and flair,
But watch out! They're slippery in mid-air!

A whale joins in with a booming sound,
His laughter echoes round and round,
They all crash down, it's a silly scene,
Underwater chaos, like a dream!

With bubbles bursting all around,
They celebrate without a bound,
This underwater party, wild and free,
No place like this in the big blue sea!

Flickers in the Midnight Sea

Beneath the waves, sparkles ignite,
Tiny fish dart, such a delight,
While deep-sea critters form a line,
They shimmy and shake, feeling just fine.

A lanternfish gives a glowy wink,
While the starfish sways in a pinky pink,
With every flicker and every swirl,
They twirl around in a watery whirl.

A jellyfish floats like a graceful balloon,
Its crown catches laughter, a silvery tune,
The ocean floor giggles, waves do a spin,
As mollusks chuckle, inviting the din.

What a sight, what a scene,
As the midnight sea throws a party routine,
Laughter bubbles under the foam,
For every creature, this sea is their home!

Timeless Rhythm of the Deep

In the deep where the rhythms beat,
A fish parade shuffles their feet,
With fins like flags, they strut and sway,
Turning the ocean into a cabaret.

Crab with a hat leads the fun,
While shrimp do the cha-cha, everyone!
The coral gardens burst into song,
As the seaweed sways, they all sing along.

A dolphin darts, twirling with glee,
Her laughter makes waves with such energy,
As clownfish juggle rainbow pearls,
Creating a splash that twirls and twirls.

In this underwater musical delight,
Every creature dances with all their might,
With laughter echoing through the deep,
They celebrate joy, no time for sleep!

Sway Beneath the Surface

In the depths where the odd ones play,
A creature sways in a comical way.
With wiggly arms and a curious glance,
Tripping through currents, it starts a dance.

Bubbles burst with a giggle or two,
As fish pause and join in the view.
A tangle of limbs that flails and whirls,
A marvelous sight to delight all the pearls.

Ebb and Flow of the Tentacles

Tentacles waving like a clumsy parade,
In a whirlpool of laughter where no plans are made.
They twist and they twirl with a slap and a splash,
Sending fish sideways in a colorful flash.

With every retreat, there's a giggling chase,
An octopus trying to keep up the pace.
Underwater antics, a slippery race,
In the ocean's embrace, they frolic with grace.

The Deep Blue Cadence

A rhythm emerges from the depths unknown,
With jive in the water, their dance is well shown.
The tempo of surf leads the way to the fun,
As buoyant beats pulse under the sun.

Each twist and each turn sends bubbles in flight,
A wobbly performance, a dizzy delight.
The seaweed sways to their silly charade,
All critters amused in this aquatic parade.

Dance of the Ink Clouds

Inky swirls paint the ocean's bright floor,
As creatures cavort and the laughter will soar.
With a splash and a giggle, they dart all around,
Creating a scene that's hilariously bound.

As clouds of dark ink play hide-and-seek,
The dolphins dive deeply, tickling their cheek.
A spectacle splashes through bubbles and foam,
In the dance of the deep, they all find a home.

Tangled in the Abyss

In the depths where sea creatures meet,
A tangled mess of eight, oh what a feat!
They twist and coil, a comical sight,
Fins and tentacles dance in the light.

Bubbles rise up with each little jig,
A party of clams and a two-legged pig.
Who leads the waltz, who follows the groove?
Not even the jellyfish can help but move!

They giggle and splash, causing a ruckus,
With flips and spins, oh, what a circus!
Octopus grins, his colors ablaze,
As fish tap along in a wobbly craze.

But beware the tickles, the mushy surprise,
As they whirl and twirl under ocean skies.
With laughter as loud as the waves that crash,
They party all night, in a splashy bash!

Inked Whispers of the Deep

On the ocean floor, a secret so bold,
Whispers of ink and stories untold.
A slippery sprite with a penchant for jokes,
Tricks all the fish and tickles the folks.

One day he scribbles a note in the tides,
Confusion abounds, oh, where it resides!
Fish swarm in circles, looking for clues,
While the squid chuckles, oh, how they do lose!

Swirls of black paint, an artistic delight,
Creating his canvas, both day and night.
Turtles get lost in his inky embrace,
As starfish join in, all beg to take space.

When laughter erupts from the sea creatures near,
You know it's the squid who brought all the cheer.
With each little flick of his tentacled hand,
He turns ocean depths to a comedy band.

Ocean's Rhythm and Tentacle Twirl

To the beat of the waves, the sea creatures sway,
Tentacles flailing to an underwater ballet.
The octopus winks with a twist of his arm,
As dolphins chime in with their laughable charm.

Splashing and flapping with joy in each whirl,
With friends all around, they tumble and twirl.
A mermaid with braids sings the funniest tune,
While crabs take the lead in a comedic monsoon.

A seahorse giggles, caught up in the fun,
As fish blow bubbles, dancing under the sun.
Every creature grins, odd shapes in a line,
Joining together, all feeling divine.

When the day ends, and laughter runs deep,
The dance doesn't fade, it's the catch of the week.
With each splash and wiggle, together they whirl,
In the ocean's embrace, it's a comical swirl!

The Cephalopod's Serenade

In a sea of giggles where turtles do glide,
A cephalopod croons with his tentacles wide.
He strums on a shell, with a twinkly pluck,
As fish come along, oh, they're really in luck!

With melodies bright that shimmy and sway,
He tickles their fins in a musical spray.
The clownfish parade with their colorful dance,
Who knew the sea would give such a chance?

Jellyfish shimmer, casting light on the fun,
Bobbing and weaving, oh look at them run!
A tale of a squid, serenading his crew,
While octopuses clap, setting rhythms anew.

As nighttime envelops with stars shining bright,
The ocean holds magic, a whimsical sight.
With laughter and music, it's a festive affair,
In the heart of the sea, joy hangs in the air!

Murmurs in the Brine

Bubbles rise in twilight's glow,
Tentacles sway, putting on a show.
With wiggly friends in the evening tide,
They giggle and wiggle, side by side.

A clam outburst, the crowd's delight,
Shells clap together with all their might.
The jellyfish jive, glowing so bright,
An underwater party, what a sight!

Crabs wearing shades, strut down the lane,
While seaweed sways in a silly chain.
An octopus juggles with flair and ease,
A game of catch with swimming peas!

With currents swirling, the laughter flows,
In the ocean's embrace, anything goes.
Drifting along, they sing a tune,
For in the brine, they dance 'til noon.

Ballet of the Bright Creatures

Underwater stage, a scene so grand,
Creatures pirouette, as planned.
Seahorses twirl in a delicate line,
While clownfish giggle, feeling divine.

The starfish flop with ungraceful flair,
Caught in a net, they pretend to care.
With sea turtles gliding, so slow and wise,
Puffers puff up, a big surprise!

A crab takes a bow, quite sure of his role,
As the tides gently sway, playing their soul.
In currents of laughter, joy isn't rare,
Ballet unfolds, everywhere!

Anemones sway in a rhythm divine,
As colors clash in a dance so fine.
In this aquatic realm, pure delight,
Creatures galore, shining so bright!

Echoes of the Deep

Flippers flicker, a splashy cheer,
Echoes bounce back, far and near.
Fish chatting about the latest news,
Underwater gossip with squid-like views.

A dolphin's giggle, a whale's loud song,
Echoes in harmony, where all belong.
Sardines schooling in choreographed lines,
Making waves with their silly designs.

Clownfish trade jokes, oh what a scene,
While crabs tell tales of the seaweed queen.
In the depths, the laughter never ends,
With each bubble burst, the joy extends.

As lanternfish flash their disco lights,
The ocean's stage hosts magical sights.
With playful whispers, the currents tease,
In watery halls, they dance with ease.

Rhapsody in Blue Waves

Rolling tides hum a carefree tune,
Beneath the waves where fish commune.
Crab and shrimp in a silly race,
Through coral gardens, they embrace space.

An orchestra plays with bubbles and sound,
As sea sponges wiggle, round and round.
Tangled in laughter, they spin and glide,
With a frothy splash, they take pride.

A seagull squawks, joining the fun,
As underwater antics have just begun.
With fins a-flip and tails a-swish,
Each creature strives for the swiftest wish.

In a watery world where joy spills free,
Colors collide in a raucous spree.
As every splash tells a story anew,
Beneath blue waves, laughter rings true.

The Flowing Moonlit Dance

Under the moon's soft glowing light,
Tentacles wiggling, oh what a sight!
Swaying to rhythms from deep down below,
The ocean chuckles at the show.

Giggling fish join in the spree,
As jellyfish twirl so gracefully.
Crabs clap their claws, keeping the beat,
While seahorses prance on tiny feet.

A dolphin leaps, caught in the fun,
With laughter echoing, just begun.
Stars twinkle above, what a delightful scene,
In this ocean party, everyone's keen!

So come, take a dive, join in the cheer,
The underwater gala is waiting here.
With each splash and wiggle, the silliness grows,
In the moonlit embrace, anything goes!

Choreographed by the Tide

Beneath the waves where the seaweed swings,
Crabs are the dancers, oh, the joy it brings!
Frisky fish twirl in their shiny attire,
While octopuses spin, as if they conspire.

A wave rolls in, cascades with a laugh,
Seagulls join in, it's a raucous half-staff.
Puffers puff up, trying to impress,
And everyone's wearing their best sea-dress.

The starfish clap in their own funky way,
As turtles groove to the tide's sway.
A conga line forms, stretching along,
In this briny bazaar, the silliness is strong!

So come ride the swell, let laughter impart,
An oceanic frolic, a splashy good start.
With friendship and fins, join the aquatic parade,
In this watery world, magic is made!

Harmonies of the Sea Floor

Down by the reef where the corals are bright,
Giggling turtles share secrets at night.
Clownfish chuckle, dodging the rays,
In a rhythm of bubbles, they sway and they play.

Blowfish puffs out, thinking he's grand,
Quotes wisdom from shellfish, a wise little band.
Anemones wave, playing peekaboo,
The giggling narwhals join in too!

They twirl and they whirl in a waterside bash,
Waving their fins, oh! A splash and a splash!
Tangs laugh loudly, it's a vibrant display,
As the sea floor hums to the tune of play.

So let's join the chorus, a sing-along glee,
Where laughter floats freely, under the sea.
With each ripple and wave, the fun never ends,
In the ocean's embrace, where mischief transcends!

Synchronicity of the Sirens

Hear the call of the waves, a whimsical tune,
As sirens giggle beneath the bright moon.
They twirl through the kelp with great flair,
While fish gather 'round, all too aware.

A seahorse stumbles, loses its grace,
As the dolphins all laugh, enjoying the chase.
Mermaids splash, a bubbly delight,
Chasing their tails in the soft moonlight.

The ocean's pure laughter flows with the tide,
As starry-eyed crabs join in with pride.
Together they frolic, hearts full of glee,
Creating a symphony, wild and free.

So come take the plunge, immerse in the fun,
With the creatures of sea, every heart is won.
In this watery wonder, it's a playful spree,
In the arms of the ocean, all spirits agree!

Twists of Tentacles in Twilight

Under the moon's playful glow,
Tentacles twirl, oh what a show!
With ink and laughter, they sway,
Creating mischief, come what may.

Bubbles burst in a silly spree,
Giggling fish join in with glee.
Cephalopod boogie, flailing about,
Who knew sea creatures could dance, no doubt?

Bright coral reefs start to cheer,
As the squids spin without fear.
In this aquatic ballet so grand,
Joyful jigs in splashes of sand.

So if you're diving in the night,
Expect a show—what a delight!
With twists and turns, take a chance,
Join the fun in their sea dance!

Fluid Movements Across the Sea Floor

On the seafloor, they glide and glide,
With swishes and swirls, they take pride.
A slippery shimmy, they bubble with glee,
Who knew that squids loved to dance so free?

With a flick of a fin, they twist and twirl,
Celebrating the underwater swirl.
Stars of the ocean, they show off their tricks,
Calamari cabarets full of slick flicks.

Crabs clap their claws in rhythmic cheer,
Joining the fun with a cheerful leer.
Even the starfish join in for a jig,
Flopping about, feeling quite big!

As the tides rise and fall, they choreograph,
Crazy pirouettes that make you laugh.
So, dive into laughter under the waves,
Where all of the sea life misbehaves!

Beneath the Currents: A Silken Waltz

Beneath rippling waves of silvery sheen,
A dance unfolds, an aquatic scene.
With friends frolicking in a grand embrace,
Squids lead the way, in a fluid race.

Using their arms like ribbons in flight,
They spin and they twirl in sheer delight.
With every shimmy, they gather their fans,
Moving like music, adjusting their plans.

The shells sway along, in a soft, sweet trance,
As all of the critters get caught in the dance.
Shrimp tap their toes with a joyful sound,
While dolphins cheer on, spinning all around.

In this wavy world, laughter flows wide,
Where tentacles twine and nothing can hide.
So come take a peek at the playtime below,
Where the squids have a ball, putting on a show!

When Shadows Swim

As shadows swim in the ocean's embrace,
Tentacle games, a quirky race.
With splashes of ink and bubbly delight,
They frolic and giggle throughout the night.

Jellyfish jiggle in soft, glowing lights,
Gaining their groove as they float into sights.
Squids swirl around in audacious flair,
Lighting up the water with fun everywhere.

A clam joins the party, opening wide,
To catch all the action, how they abide!
Crustaceans chuckle as they clap and cheer,
Celebrating moments of joy that endear.

As laughter echoes through depths of the sea,
Join in the revelry, carefree, and free.
No worries tonight, it's all in good fun,
With shadows and squids, let the hilarity run!

Undercurrents of Desire

Beneath the waves, a wiggly friend,
Spinning and twisting, oh what a blend!
A tickle of tentacles, a slippery tease,
He winks at the fish, saying, "Just feel the breeze!"

With laughter and bubbles, they play hide and seek,
In a world of delights, where mischief's unique.
Jellyfish giggle in rhythmic delight,
As crabs join the fray, all dancing in sight!

The seahorses prance in this whimsical sea,
While starfish look on, feeling quite glee.
It's a party of color, of jiggles and swirls,
Where the ocean's a stage for aquatic twirls!

But watch out, dear friend, for the hungry shark,
He's known for his moves, but not for his spark.
With a slip and a slide, they dash to and fro,
In this tide of giggles, it's all about flow!

The Pulse of the Deep

Down where the currents are full of surprise,
A belly flop creature with big googly eyes.
He dances with bubbles, oh what a sight,
In a waltz of the waves, a humorous flight!

The fish roll their eyes, they just can't believe,
That a creature with eight arms can truly achieve.
With flails and with flops, he takes to the floor,
In a swirling parade, there's always more!

The turtles chuckle, the dolphins all cheer,
As he twirls in the tide, filled with whimsy, not fear.
Each twist tells a tale, each splash draws a grin,
The ocean's alive; let the fun times begin!

So come join the frolic, don't miss out for long,
Where the rhythm of sea life makes everyone strong.
For under the waves, pure joy can be found,
In the pulse of the deep, we're all tightly wound!

Odysseys in Gelatinous Tides

In a jiggly realm, a festival thrives,
With creatures so slimy, they wiggle like jives.
Each flip of the flippers brings laughter anew,
As they bob and they weave, just like a funny crew!

Unbeknownst to squid, who then takes a glide,
A dance party starts on a slimy slide.
With jellybeans bouncing, and sauces galore,
They twirl like spaghetti, it's hard to ignore!

Crabs crab-walk with style, giving clumsy high-fives,
While eels twist and shout, leading jigs in their dives.
The seaweed sways gently, to beats from below,
In a wobbly waltz, where the silliness flows!

So gather your friends, it's a night of pure glee,
Underneath the moonlight, where all spirits roam free.
In this odyssey wild, with laughter and glee,
We swirl in the gel, as happy as can be!

Echoes of the Deep Sea Waltz

In the depths of the ocean, a rhythm takes flight,
As creatures declare it's dance party night!
With echoes of chuckles and splashes of fun,
They twirl in the darkness, till the dance is done!

A squid on the move, with a flair and a spin,
Makes everybody laugh, as he wiggles in.
The fish form a line, with scales that all shine,
In a conga of joy, oh how they entwine!

A chorus of sea sounds, they jingle and jive,
As the playful sea turtles join in the dive.
In a whirl of bright colors, they frolic and sway,
Creating a spectacle that brightens their day!

So let the sea bubble, let the laughter not cease,
For here in this dance, we all find our peace.
With echoes of joy in the salty sea breeze,
The deep sea waltz is our ticket to ease!

Shadows of the Gulf

In the depths where shadows play,
Tentacles twirl in a ballet.
Laughter bubbles from the sea,
Wiggling legs, oh what glee!

A pirate ship drifts by with cheer,
"Is that a dance?" we shout, "Oh dear!"
But squids just grin and make a splash,
As they perform their squishy bash!

With ink like paint, they doodle bright,
Turning the ocean into a sight.
Bubbles burst with each silly twirl,
Underwater giggles, oh what a whirl!

So if you're near and hear a squeal,
It's just the squids making a deal.
Join in the fun, don't be shy,
And watch the dance beneath the sky!

Currents of the Unseen

Beneath the waves, the mischief brews,
Tentacles tease with quirky cues.
They tie themselves in knots and loops,
While fish swim by in silly groups.

With a swish and a whoosh, they chase the light,
Flipping and flopping, pure delight.
All the bubbles dance in cheer,
As squids make faces that bring a sneer!

The clams clap shells, the crabs all cheer,
When squids pirouette with no real fear.
The jellyfish wobble, join in the fun,
And dance along 'til the day is done!

So when you're down at the ocean shore,
Listen closely for laughter galore.
The currents hold secrets, if you dare,
To join the dance that lives in the air!

Surrender to the Unknown

In a world that sways and spins,
Squids invite you; let's begin!
With a splash and a wink, they take the lead,
Whirling about, it's all you need!

The octopuses roll their eyes with glee,
As squids perform a jig, wild and free.
"Join us now," they seem to say,
"Embrace the unknown, come out to play!"

Ink clouds flutter as laughter blooms,
Creating colorful underwater rooms.
With flips and flops, they surge along,
Their dance makes even fish sing a song!

So heed the call of this lively show,
Let down your guard, just let it flow.
Join the squids in their cheerful spree,
And surrender to fun beneath the sea!

Whirling Wonders of the Tide

When moonlight twinkles on the tide,
Squids are out to take a ride.
They swirl and twirl, with ink in hand,
Creating paintings across the sand.

With a flap and a flop, they twist and bend,
Inviting sea creatures, every friend.
"A little dance? Come join our craze!"
They giggle and wiggle in many ways.

The clumsy dolphins join in too,
With cartwheels and spins, they laugh, who knew?
Together they create a swirling parade,
Where every move brings laughter displayed!

So next time you stroll by the shore,
Take a moment, you'll find much more.
Join the squids in their winding waltz,
And share in their joy, without a fault!

Wading Through Ocean Dreams

In the depths where sea creatures leap,
An octopus wears my hat, oh so deep.
He wobbles and jigs with such flair,
Who knew squishy things could dance and care?

The fish giggle as they swirl around,
While jellyfish float, they're never quite bound.
I trip on a dolphin, slip on a wave,
Each splash ignites laughter, how the sea saves!

A crab claps its claws, marching with glee,
While seahorses twirl, oh, can't you see?
I join in their fun, the rhythm so bright,
With a splash, I take flight under moonlight!

In this ocean of giggles, oh what a sight,
Where the silly sea critters dance through the night.
I laugh with my friends, the tide is our stage,
In this wading wonder, we all share a page!

Currents of the Choreographed Unknown

Bubbles rise up like notes of a song,
As the seaweed sways, I must sing along.
A crab's tango pulls me into the scene,
In this underwater party, life's never routine.

The eels do a shuffle, wiggly and sleek,
While fish form a train, oh, what a technique!
A clam claps its shells, keeping the beat,
And I can't help but sway in this dance so sweet.

Whirling with whirlpools, I twist and I twirl,
With octopuses lending their arms for a whirl.
Flapping my fins, I'm part of the crew,
In this absurd ballet of oceanic view!

With laughter and bubbles, life's never a bore,
In this sea of confusion, there's always much more.
So grab your flippers, my friends, don't be shy,
Join the currents unknown, and let's dance, oh my!

Whispers in the Waves

In the hush of the sea where secrets reside,
Giggling mussels peek out from their hide.
They whisper soft tales of bubbles gone wild,
As the starfish spins round, it's truly beguiled.

Coral reefs chuckle, colors so bright,
While plankton jive by the pale moonlight.
The sea sponges poker-faced, wave after wave,
Pretending to be statues, oh how they misbehave!

A dance in the shallows with crabs in accord,
Ballet of barnacles, never ignored.
With a flip and a flop, the laughter erupts,
As an echoing sea turtle tries to interrupt.

So let's heed the call of the waves' merry song,
For in this watery world, we all belong.
Whispers and giggles fill the salty air,
In the sphere of the ocean, let's shake off our care!

Swaying with Shadows Beneath

Beneath the surface where shadows collide,
I dance with the creatures, oh what a ride!
Anemones sway in a rhythm divine,
While the snails do the cha-cha, sipping on brine.

The octopus grins with eight arms to share,
As the flatfish flops, unaware of the stare.
A mackerel winks with a flick of its tail,
While I twirl and I twist, oh how I prevail!

In this bubbling ballet where giggles abound,
We paddle and jiggle, turning the ground.
A dance full of folly, with joy all around,
We break through the silence, with laughter we're crowned!

So, sway with the shadows, let's leap through the tides,
In this quirky lagoon, where humor resides.
With a wink and a splash, we'll dance 'til the end,
In the sea's great embrace, where silly times blend!

Currents of Color in the Deep Blue

In waters swirling, bright and bold,
Tentacles twirl, a sight to behold.
With colors flashing, laughter rings,
As fish join in with silly flings.

An octopus dons a hat so bright,
Waving at crabs, what a funny sight!
They giggle and dance, lose their way,
Tumbling together in the spray.

A splash and a dive, a jolly spree,
Cephalopod antics under the sea.
With jellyfish friends bouncing around,
Creating chaos in joyful sound.

So let the currents twist and sway,
With a wink and a whirl, they play all day.
In this world of color and cheer,
The ocean's laughter is all we hear.

The Elegance of Eight Arms

With graceful swirls and a floppy glide,
An eight-armed dancer takes the tide.
Spinning in circles, a sight so fine,
With each wobbly move, how they shine!

A clam on stage, looking quite grand,
As our hero waves, isn't it planned?
"Oh look, a pirate!" yells fish in fright,
Throwing seaweed, what a comical sight!

Bubbles burst forth with a giggly chime,
The mollusk twirls in rhythm and rhyme.
A sea star claps, they applaud with glee,
For the elegant show in the deep blue sea.

Jellyfish float by, making waves,
While shrimp join in with wiggly graces.
In this watery ballroom, laughter is near,
As they all join in, each one a dear.

Nautical Night: A Gallant Encounter

Underneath the stars, a party brews,
With sea critters donning their fanciest hues.
A squid in a tux, with style unmatched,
With comedic charm, the night's dispatched.

He steps on the sand, what a grand debut,
With a flip and a flop, the crowd goes woo!
Crabs crack jokes, their pincers a-clack,
As laughter erupts, they share a snack.

A dolphin sings, with a cheeky wink,
While sea turtles glide, giving a think.
"Can you dance?" asks a shrimp, feeling bold,
"Yes, watch me spin!" is the squid's retold.

The waves join in, creating the sound,
As all watery beings scatter around.
In the moonlight's glow, they twirl and swim,
The night full of giggles, the Merriest whim!

A Dip into Seafoam Dances

In frothy waves where laughter lives,
Squid and friends prepare their jives.
With splishy-splashy, flappy fins,
They twirl and giggle, where fun begins.

A crustacean laughs as it takes a bath,
Slipping and sliding, it finds its path.
The seaweed sways to a bubbly beat,
As octopus joins, making it sweet!

Castles of sand rise in the foam,
Where every creature feels at home.
Fish in bow ties, they follow the lead,
With bubbles that tickle, they dance with speed!

They tumble through tides in joyful delight,
Creating a splash, oh what a sight!
Under the waves, where dreams are found,
A party in motion, so lively and sound.

Ballet of the Hidden Depths

In the depths where the seaweed sways,
A troupe of cephalopods play,
They twirl in a ballet quite absurd,
With pirouettes that seem unheard.

One's wearing a hat made of shells,
While another rings marine bells,
They leap and they glide, no time to eat,
With a jellyfish joining for a treat.

A crab plays the role of the judge,
Clapping his claws, he won't budge,
While fish gather round to critique,
On their performance, so unique!

With mollusks cheering from the side,
In this oceanic joyride,
They dance, they spin, in a mismatched crew,
And giggles erupt in the aquatic blue!

Tentacle Tango at Dusk

As the sun dips low in the sea,
Tentacles twist with glee,
Eight-legged partners entwine and sway,
In a tango that's wild and gay.

A group of fish starts to prance,
They join in the ocean's silly dance,
With bubbles bursting, they flip and race,
Try to keep up in this funny chase.

A seahorse shimmies, trying to flip,
While a squid takes a comical dip,
They twirl and whirl, round and round,
In the warm waters where joy is found.

With a wink from a starfish on a stone,
It's the best jig that's ever been known,
In the twilight, they laugh and sing,
Under the waves, a shiny fling!

Luminescence in the Blue Abyss

Deep in the ocean where it's dark,
Creatures glow with a quirky spark,
A light show of colors, strange and bright,
Making the water a glorious sight.

A squid with a glow, a dazzling show,
Bounces around in a flowing flow,
While a clownfish cracks a silly joke,
With laughter bubbling, it's no hoax.

A lanternfish dims, then shines anew,
As if to say, 'Join in the crew!'
In the depths, they sparkle and play,
Creating the wildest cabaret.

With each flash, a giggle slips through,
The darkness hums with lights that woo,
In this abyss where smiles bloom,
A friendship dances, lighting the gloom!

Whirlpools of Creaturely Grace

In swirling pools of warm embrace,
Creatures gather to flaunt their grace,
With dolphins diving, putting on flair,
They spin and flip, full of dare.

A playful seal juggles some fish,
While others buckle, granting a wish,
The octopus paints, with colors galore,
An art show that leaves you wanting more!

Together they whirl in splashes and sprays,
In a contest of talent, no time for malaise,
With shrimp as the audience, clapping with zest,
It's a dinner show that's simply the best!

As the tide ebbs, and laughter takes flight,
In whirlpools of joy, every heart feels light,
For in this deep world, where fun is a race,
Creatures unite with a quirky grace!

Spirals of the Blue

In the ocean's vast embrace,
A creature twirls with grace,
Tentacles flail, a wobbly show,
Who knew fish could dance so slow?

With ink clouds puffed, it takes a spin,
Giggling fish join in the din,
A wiggly party, all in jest,
Who knew the deep could laugh the best?

Bubble rings float with delight,
The ocean floor just feels so light,
As clownfish chuckle, sneaking peeks,
At this odd dance of twisted freaks!

With a splash and a flick, they prance,
In this underwater funky dance,
Where silliness reigns with each new twirl,
Oh what a joy, this watery whirl!

Cosmic Currents of Color

In the depths where oddities bloom,
A creature paints the ocean's room,
With hues that spin and swirl around,
Vertices of laughter can be found.

Tentacles whirl like ribbons bright,
Funky moves in the pale moonlight,
Dancers jiggle, bubbles burst,
Underwater giggles—a joyful thirst!

A disco ball made of seashells gleam,
While jellyfish sway like they're in a dream,
The vibrant dance floor, it never ends,
With dancing pals, the best of friends!

As currents flow in a foolish spree,
The sea's a stage, what glee to see,
With pops of color and jolly cheer,
Who knew the ocean held such beer?

Serpent of the Sea

Behold the snake that wiggles by,
With a silly grin, oh my, oh my!
It slithers slow, then quickens the beat,
In a wobbly jig, it can't be beat!

With fish all laughing in their schools,
It breaks the rules, it bends the jewels,
A serpentine twist in a shimmering show,
Dancing to music only they know!

The dolphins dive with playful yaps,
As the serpent spins amidst the claps,
Tails flying high, in waves they frolic,
In this twisty sea, all is symbolic!

For life is funny when it's all a game,
Who knew the deep would bring such fame?
With laughter rising like ocean foam,
Together they all find their home!

Euphoria in the Green Depths

In emerald waters, laughter flows,
Where an odd little creature quietly glows,
With frisky motions, it twirls about,
In this jolly world, there's never doubt!

Seaweed sways like a giggling friend,
As the playful prankster starts to bend,
With swirls and swishes, it strikes a pose,
In the green depths where silliness grows!

The clams clap shells in a rhythmic delight,
As the octopus boogies into the night,
With jellyfish joining the swirl of fun,
In this underwater rave, everyone!

So twirl and twist, let the tides bring cheer,
For trivial joys are always near,
In oceans deep, let laughter spread,
Join the green depths, dance till you're wed!

Colorful Echoes in the Depths

In the ocean's vast embrace,
A creature spins with flair,
With arms like flying ribbons,
It twirls without a care.

A wink from forty eyes,
It juggles fish for fun,
They giggle in delight,
Oh what a sight, oh what a run!

Splashing colors here and there,
In playful leaps and bounds,
Watch out for that water spray,
As laughter echoes 'round!

From bubble-blowing tricks,
To pirouettes so bright,
This funny, floppy dancer,
Brings joy to day and night.

Tidal Twirls of Time

Flipping through the waves,
A cephalopod takes flight,
With twists that shimmer sunbeams,
And sparkles pure and bright.

Dancing on the sandy stage,
With friends both big and small,
They laugh and share their secrets,
Oh, what a merry call!

The tides begin to change,
With currents swift and free,
This clumsy show of wiggles,
Is pure hilarity.

Time drifts in the ocean blue,
Where giggles rule the day,
In a grand aquatic show,
That splashes fears away.

The Seabed's Silent Waltz

Beneath the waves, a secret kept,
A dance that goes unseen,
With mystic moves and silly twirls,
In shades of seaweed green.

They glide and slide with joyous glee,
In circles oh so wide,
A ballet of the curious,
Where laughter takes a ride.

Tentacles entwined in laughter,
They tickle starfish' feet,
The crabs join in the fun and games,
Amid the ocean's beat.

When bubbles burst in giggles here,
And jellyfish do sway,
This silent waltz of whimsy,
Will brighten up your day!

Ethereal Motion of the Tentacles

With arms that stretch like spaghetti,
In rolls and flips they play,
This ink-squirting roguish sprite,
Is quite the comical display.

Whirling 'round in playful chaos,
In currents of the sea,
With every twist and coil they do,
Bring endless fun and glee.

Bubbles rise like laughter's song,
As creatures join the round,
In this ocean party bash,
Where silly moves abound.

Ethereal motions flit and frolic,
Through depths so full of cheer,
This giggly creature's antics,
Will draw the whole world near.

Fathomless Acrobatics

With tentacles flailing, oh what a sight,
The creature spins round in the pale moonlight.
It juggles some fish, quite a curious feat,
While seagulls all snicker at its wobbly beat.

Bubbles are bursting from laughter and fun,
The ocean's a circus where all are well-sunned.
A twist and a turn, in its slippery trend,
The applause of the waves, it shall gladly send.

It's a noodle and squiggle, a float and a flip,
A marine extravaganza, not to let slip.
When friends gather 'round, with popcorn in tow,
They'll cheer on the acrobat stealing the show.

And though we all ponder if squids can truly play,
We laugh as they dance 'neath the soft ocean spray.
Their antics immortal, a tale to recount,
Of delightful oddities that splash all about.

Grasping at Seafoam

Dare to reach out where the froth meets the tide,
A squid tries its luck, with a wink and a glide.
It stretches its arms, oh the joy and the glee,
But catches a wave, oh where can it be?

Flipping through bubbles, in a sea of delight,
It swirls and it twirls, what a comical sight.
"Seaweed for lunch?" it fervently thought,
But a crab scuttled past, with a grumpy retort.

It feigned innocence, blushing a blue,
Then squirted some ink, like a painter would do.
With splatters and smudges, it claimed the deep sea,
"My masterpiece is just what I need to be free!"

So, grasping at seafoam, it wiggled with charm,
In antics and laughter, it brought no alarm.
The ocean now echoes with its silly cheer,
As everyone watches, with glee and with beer!

Medley of Mysteries

In the depths of the blue, where wonders abide,
An eight-armed performer, with mischief and pride.
It beckons the fish, come join in the fun,
For a wobbly jig under warmth from the sun.

The starfish look puzzled, the crabs roll their eyes,
As the squid starts a sonnet, a chorus of sighs.
"What is that rhythm?" a turtle asks slow,
"I think it's just happy!" snickers a whelk low.

With movements so funny, and splashes in tow,
The sea creatures gather to join in the show.
It flips and it flops, with flair and with zest,
In a medley of jiggles, it truly is blessed.

So round and around, they continue to swirl,
In a whirlpool of laughter, the waters unfurl.
From frogging to twinkling, their hearts full of cheer,
A symphony waltzing that all want to hear.

Reverie in the Current

Under the ripples, where mischief does dwell,
A squid dreams of dancing, it's under a spell.
With every soft wave, it glimmers and glides,
Spinning tales of whimsy, where humor abides.

Through lavender seaweed, it weaves like a pro,
With each twist and turn, it puts on a show.
A flurry of laughter erupts from the sand,
As the octopus cheers, giving it a hand.

It rifles through bubbles, both silly and bright,
In a reverie deep, swimming all through the night.
The sand dollars giggle at each quirky cha-cha,
While clams hold their shells, saying "Ha-ha!"

The tide keeps on pushing, but never feels done,
For every splash echoes, a ticket to fun.
A brief, wild moment, now lost in the tide,
But memories linger, laughter still wide.

www.ingramcontent.com/pod-product-compliance
Lightning Source LLC
Chambersburg PA
CBHW060113230426
43661CB00003B/170